⏱ SECONDS AWAY FROM...

Outstanding Leadership

"Molly Harvey has created something amazing, emotional, inspiring and of huge value. It will change readers' lives. I don't know how she does it but thank God she did."
Sir Eric Peacock

"Molly Harvey has provided poignant and powerful leadership tools that are applicable professionally and personally. Her practical framework is a must read for those who aspire to lead where others have not gone. Molly's style of engagement is contagious."
Louise Griffith, Passion & Greatness Coach, One Shining Light

"When time is the most precious daily commodity for leaders, it's rare for us to devour a management book from cover to cover, but this little gem is such an enjoyable and useful read, so full of practical, personal tips, that I found I couldn't put it down! It provokes reflection, demands positive action and inspires possibility!"
Jeanette Kehoe-Perkinson, Interim HR Director, Iceland Foods

"Seconds away from outstanding leadership gives you a mentor and a coach on the corner of your desk. Those who find themselves thrust into a leadership role will see that it's not a science, it's all about behaviour. For those of us who have been on the leadership road for some time this book comes into its own when we have that slip in confidence, graze our knees and need that help getting back up and on the road to lead the great team we have been blessed with."
Paul Naylon, Managing Director, NOV Mono

"This book is a complete lesson in effective leadership – everything you need to make you the best leader you can be – just add personal commitment and you're there!"
Julie Fadden, Director, South Liverpool Housing Association

Molly Harvey

 SECONDS AWAY FROM...

Outstanding Leadership

First published in 2012 by
Infinite Ideas Limited
36 St Giles
Oxford
OX1 3LD
United Kingdom
www.infideas.com

A CIP catalogue record for this book is available from the British Library

ISBN 978-1-906821-78-4
Brand and product names are trademarks or registered trademarks of their
respective owners.

Cover designed by Darren Hayball
Text designed and typeset by Nicki Averill
Printed and bound by CPI Group (UK) Ltd, Croydon, CR0 4YY

'Leadership is all about presence and impact;
and how you show up every moment of the day.'

Molly

Contents

Acknowledgements

I am most appreciative of the many people who have offered tips and ideas for this little book.

Thank you to Sir Eric Peacock; you are an inspiration to me. Also thank you to Joe Adams from the Academy for Chief Executives; I value the wisdom and the stories you have shared.

I especially want to thank Richard Burton from Infinite Ideas for taking a chance and believing in me and also my agent Brendan O'Connor from The London Speaker Bureau, who continues to encourage me.

Special thanks to my PA Sylvia Morgan, who is enormously skilled at what she does.

My family means the world to me. Thank you Neil, Declan and Siobhan for your continuous love and support; I love you all more than words can say.

Finally but most importantly, thank you to my best friend in Minnesota, USA, Louise Griffith for your listening ear.

Where the 'Seconds away from...' idea came from

The 'Seconds away from...' concept came about one day over a cup of coffee with a leading authority in social media. His name is Bryan Adams and he is the creator of a funky company called Ph.Creative (**www.Ph.Creative.com**).

Bryan, thank you for challenging me and believing in me. You rock and you are an outstanding leader.

Introduction

'Leadership is all about the ability to show up and allow everyone around you to step forth.'
Molly Harvey

Since 1993, I have been running various leadership programmes around the world, and many challenges within our world today stem in part from a leadership that is ill-prepared to deal with the current complexity of a fast changing world. The old systems of power are crumbling around the world. Corporates and institutions are crying out for a new kind of leadership.

In 2008, I had the privilege to be one of twenty people picked by Dr Jean Houston and the United Nations Development Programme to undergo Social Artist training in Ashland, Oregon. The new outstanding leader, or as Dr Houston calls the Social Artist, dares to lead with courage, vision, imagination and heart. Now is the time for real and positive change in this world. We don't need any more membership cards as the world is full of statistics; we now need leaders to be real, honest and transparent.

How the book is structured

This book includes simple and relevant tips on leadership that you can glance through in seconds, or go back and ponder on in depth.

We are living in a world of information overload and we want information in seconds rather than hours.

To help you quickly learn the six steps to becoming an outstanding leader, I have organised the book into six chapters.

Chapter one looks at self leadership and how you deal with things day-to-day. Each chapter is broken down into several pages of tips and practical ideas that you can implement into your life and workplace.

The next few chapters are all about what it takes to be an outstanding leader and the disciplines involved.

The final chapter focuses on action and what actions you need to take every day as a leader.

Each section also includes a 'seconds to ponder' page and an actions list that can be completed at the end of each chapter.

You may want to read the book through once just to get a feel for the six steps and then go back and ponder over some of the tips covered in more depth. As you are reading, I strongly encourage you to underline and highlight sections you feel are important to you. Maybe read one chapter for thirty days and implement the tips one by one. Remember, repetition is the key to the success of many great leaders.

Molly

Presence

'Pay any price to be in the presence of extraordinary people.'
Mike Murdock

From an early age, I was able to see and feel the 'presence' of another human being. When I talk about presence I mean aliveness. It is not the things that you do, but the way you are – your 'youness'. Your presence is the way you express your definition of yourself.

I grew up on a country estate in County Waterford, owned by the Marquis of Waterford. The estate was a playground for my inner development and imagination. I realised at a very young age that a human being is a palace of many rooms, many capacities and much potential. I have since learned that in decades of research it has been found that all human beings contain inner realms but few have more than a passing acquaintance with the depth of their own presence.

Outstanding leaders project power through their presence. The human body longs for presence and the body is a language that cannot remain silent. As John O'Donohue once said, 'the human face is a miniature village of presence'.

The saddest thing in corporate life today is that too many people learn to close themselves off and treat the essence of who they are, no longer as presence but as function. The functionalist mind is only committed to maintenance and efficiency. When you diminish the presence of who you are, you diminish the presence of everyone around you.

The time has come for leaders to learn to see with their hearts first and lead from the inside out.

'May you awaken to the mystery of being here and enter the quiet immensity of your inner presence; may you experience each day as a sacred gift woven around the heart of wonder.'
John O'Donohue

Presence

Think back to a time when you were totally enchanted by someone else's presence. You were aware of every word and movement they made. Now step back and think for a moment, what does your presence say about you? Is your presence approachable? If people cannot approach you, how can they follow you?

- When you feel truly comfortable in your own skin, you show up as you truly are.

- To be an outstanding leader and lead from the inside out, you need to first get to know yourself.

- Practise letting the essence of your presence say who you truly are. No words are needed.

- The essence of your presence lingers in the room long after you have left the room.

- Presence is energy and when you are in alignment with your head, heart and belly brain, you will be aligned with what and who you truly are.

- Presence is invisible yet we can feel it.

- The presence of a leader who has stillness and contentment of heart, engenders trust.

- Presence is alive; you can feel and sense presence. It comes towards you and engages you when you connect with another human being.

- Presence is more than the way a leader walks, speaks and looks; it is something each and every one of us can sense and know, yet can never touch.

Leave your ego at the door

We all need a certain amount of ego to get out of bed in the morning.
It's very often what motivates us to a whole new level. However, ego
leadership can be very shallow as it is all about *me* and how great *I* am
as a leader. Many years ago at a National Speakers' Convention in Dallas,
Nido Qubein asked the audience a great question, 'Do you want to be
known for fame or significance?' Which would you choose?

- Learn to talk less and listen more.

- Remember that all those you meet wear huge signs around their
  necks. Those signs say 'MAKE ME FEEL IMPORTANT'.

- If you let your ego control you, that's what the world will reflect back
  to you.

- Ego is that part of you that believes human beings are all separate and
  that some are more special than others.

- True power does not promote or support powerlessness in others nor
  is it dominant, controlling or overbearing.

- Your ego very often slams on the brakes and resists change; observe
  your movements, language and actions for twenty-four hours.

- Ego seeks out all others who come under its spell, draining them of
  their life force.

- Very often we try to persuade or influence people in the way we
  like to be persuaded or influenced. Guess what? It doesn't always
  work because the differences between people are not minor, they're
  dramatic.

Be an enchanting leader

When my mother was thirty-six years old, she was given the news that she had to have all her teeth removed due to gum disease. Soon afterwards she was fitted for her new teeth. Then one day I noticed she never wore her teeth except for weddings, christenings and funerals. I was initially embarrassed and used to say, 'Mammy put your teeth in', and her reply was, 'they don't feel comfortable'. It was then I realised that my mother charmed everyone she met; she didn't need to wear teeth to be real. She created an emotional response in everyone by enchanting them with her hospitality and stories.

■ Enchanting leaders are innovators.

■ Enchanting leaders are original.

■ Enchanting leaders focus on people.

■ Enchanting leaders inspire trust.

■ Enchanting leaders begin from the end.

■ Enchanting leaders ask 'why?' and 'what?'.

■ Enchanting leaders challenge and question.

■ Enchanting leaders do the right thing.

■ Enchanting leaders are their own people.

Get out of your own way

The pessimist complains about the wind. The optimist expects it to change. The outstanding leader adjusts the sails.

Very often in life the only person who stops you from moving forward is you. Outstanding leaders learn to stop self-sabotaging, step aside and move out of their own way.

- Be an example so that others are inspired by your actions and presence.

- Step aside, create space and let others be encouraged to achieve their own greatness.

- When you get out of your own way, you will automatically come from a cooperative rather than competitive mindset.

- Stop giving advice all day long. Learn to trust your intuition, take responsibility for your decisions and teach others to do the same.

- Every day ask yourself the hard question, 'What am I here to do?' Watch yourself become a cauldron of possibility for everyone around you.

- When you get out of your own way, you will begin to look at things differently and feel and think more creatively.

- When you step aside, you allow possibility to step into your life and then, just like a rich fabric, you can weave your future from possibility.

Change your thinking

J.C. Penney once said, 'No one need live a minute longer as he is because the creator endowed us with the ability to change ourselves'. Outstanding leaders are not outstanding because of their power but because of their ability to manage their thoughts daily and empower everyone else around them.

- True success has nothing to do with what you have; it's all about where you are going.

- The more you work on your inner development, the better your outside world becomes.

- Remember you are always only one thought away from positivity.

- Only you can choose whether you think positive or negative thoughts moment to moment.

- Observe your thinking as if you are outside your body. When negative thoughts arise, simply say, 'Delete, delete, delete'.

- When we change our thinking, we automatically become aware of the opportunity around us.

- If you think it you can *be* it; if you think it you can *do* it.

- Stop thinking on the outside, start thinking on the inside.

- When the old ways are not working, change your thinking and the answers will come.

Be there for people

Outstanding leaders know that everything they accomplish happens not just because of their efforts but through the efforts of others.

I recently worked with a CEO who brought thirty of his leaders from around the world to the west of Ireland. He was a humble and quiet leader who empowered his people through action and the right words. For example, he said, 'Thank you to each and every one of you for working with me'. Notice he did not say 'working *for* me'. He was a leader who empowered his people by working with them not using his power over them.

- If you treat others the way you like to be treated, you are likely to be getting it wrong for two-thirds of the people around you. We are all different. Always make the other person your starting point and treat them the way they want to be treated.

- Outstanding leaders are excellent observers and watch the energy, language and strategy of everyone they meet.

- Rapport happens when the other person experiences sameness and feels you understand them. Then you will have their support.

- Without congruence you will be considered insincere and manipulative.

- To grow a business, we need to grow people.

- Outstanding leaders say the right thing in the right way and at the right time.

- The best way to inspire people to superior performance is to convince them by everything you do and by your daily attitude, that you wholeheartedly support them.

- True caring for people should come naturally; it should not be faked or forced.

- Remember to praise everyone around you. By knowing the strengths of those around you, you will be able to praise them in a way that matches their needs, energy, language and strategy.

Make a difference in seconds

Making a difference doesn't have to cost a lot of money. One CEO of a large multinational I have worked with personally writes a Christmas card to each employee. As there are thousands of people employed in the company, he starts signing cards in January each year.

- Leadership is all about the way you show up.

- Start today to make a difference from where you are.

- On a scale from 1 to 10, how approachable are you currently?

- The only way to open the corporate heart is to lead from your own heart today and make a difference.

- Hand write a note to three people who have made a difference in your life or order your favourite book and send it to them.

- Take time to think today of how you can do what you currently do more effectively.

- Take time to think about how you can help people in a greater way and make a real and lasting difference.

- When it comes to strategy, ponder less and take action more.

- Stop going through the motions of living; savour today and go out and make a difference.

- Money and power alone will never make you happy. You either choose to have an impact upon your environment today or your environment will define you.

- Outstanding leaders, teams and organisations are simply ordinary people who, on an daily basis, do extraordinary things that matter to them and everyone around them.

Presence within the company environment

Very often I can tell the level of morale in a company just by standing in the reception area. The reception of a company is the face it presents to the outside world. The atmosphere and décor, down to each painting on the wall, tell a story. Is the area clean, well presented and busy with creativity and activity or is the reception tired and jaded with chipped paint and fake flowers? First impressions last and say a lot about the values and ideals of the organisation.

- The furniture, colours and décor of your organisation create presence.

- Get the culture of your company right and everything else will follow.

- Brand and culture are two sides of the same coin.

- As a leader, ask yourself daily why you do what you do.

- When employees are engaged, customers are engaged.

- When employees feel they belong and enjoy their work, a sense of community grows within the workplace.

- If you don't live up to the core values of your company, they are worthless; merely a plaque on the wall of your office.

- Have the results from each team within your organisation made more visible. It creates ownership, presence and accountability.

- Stamp out the 'I don't care' attitude from your company; it causes the presence of the company environment to become stale.

Progress from good to outstanding leadership

In today's volatile economy good is no longer good enough. All leaders, no matter how charismatic or visionary they are, eventually move on or retire. Outstanding leaders move beyond 'good' to 'world-class' and create a company with values and processes that outlast their leadership. When they leave, the company will have become a visionary company that is not just successful, but also known and admired for being world-class.

- Develop humbleness and give yourself the permission to say, 'I don't know', now and again.

- Leaders are rarely the best performers so surround yourself with great talent.

- Consistently disrupt your old ways of being and embrace discomfort.

- Stay grounded, work hard and build renewal time into your diary.

- Every day do the difficult things first.

- Learn to make mistakes faster so that you can quickly turn your failures into successes.

- Nurture everyone else around you to lead.

- Become a great storyteller so that everyone around you can learn faster.

- Know when to leave; know when to quit; know when to be patient.

Develop high self-awareness as a leader

As new leaders emerge around the world, I am amazed at how self-aware they are. I got a call from the Chief Executive of a housing association about two years ago. When I went to meet her, she told me that she felt a lot of the current problems in her organisation were due to the managers not being self-aware, so she wanted to develop an emotional intelligence programme that would run throughout the organisation from the chief executive level down.

Some people were really sceptical that this would work, but the programme was reviewed monthly by various departments and the feedback and results were amazing. Communication and awareness improved dramatically within the next six months.

- High self-awareness enables you to monitor yourself and observe yourself in action.

- Outstanding leaders learn to tune into their senses – seeing, smelling, hearing, tasting, touching. It is through your senses that you will pick up information on how you are leading.

- When you become centred, you connect with yourself, as you will have an increased awareness of what is going on within yourself and your environment.

- When we develop high self-awareness, we become the person we envisage ourselves as and can shape the world to fit our perception of it.

- When we are self-aware, we are more likely to be courageous and accept that losses can also be gains in life.

- Self-aware leaders develop ways to set clear boundaries and maintain personal space, even when there is conflict.

Lead without a title

Outstanding leaders encourage and inspire each of their people to be the CEO of their own job. True leadership is beyond titles; it's where you set a great example and that inspires and influences everyone around you to do the same. A few years ago I worked with a large college in England. The principal asked to meet with me a few weeks before I did the opening keynote speech at their annual conference. Within a few minutes of meeting her, I realised she was more interested in her people their than titles. She briefed me to leave people with the message that everyone in the college mattered, from the janitor up to the professors, regardless of their job title. This was a woman who led from the front without a title.

- You don't need a title to lead by example.

- Passion, desire and commitment are more important than titles.

- Be truly excellent at what you do.

- Be responsible all of the time.

- Have the courage to follow your heart and intuition.

- Quit making excuses and take one step towards action today.

- At the end of each day ask yourself what have you done well? Where have you wasted your time?

Wisdom

Truly wise leaders not only lead in their businesses each day but also realise the importance of developing their own characters and living with ease and grace. One of the wisest leaders I have ever studied was Gandhi. To me he is the model of wisdom leadership.

One day he was getting off a train when one of his shoes fell onto the track. As the train started to move it was too late to retrieve it so he took off his other shoe and threw it on the track too. His companions were speechless and asked why he had done it. His reply was, 'Now the poor man who finds the shoe on the track will have a pair he can use.' Gandhi was clearly one of the wisest leaders who ever lived.

- Each day leave every person you come into contact with the impression of increase.

- Question everything in your life that doesn't feel right and, if necessary, let it go.

- Are you currently living your life on your terms or someone else's?

- A life well lived is doing what you love to do all day long.

- Learn to trust in your greatness; turn inside for answers instead of outside.

- Stop pushing and just be. Notice the flow in life and take action in the flow.

- Let go of always having to be right; let go of always having to know everything.

- When we stop trying to control the lives of others, we live in true harmony.

- Be humble – you will know when to let go, when to stop and when to move forward.

- When times get tough and you feel like you can no longer go on, remember, 'this too shall pass'.

Leave a wake

What kind of a wake do you create each day as you lead within your organisation? On a storyboard in our office is a picture of a giant wake taken when my family and I went on a summer vacation to Minnesota a few years ago. My business friend and fellow speaker owned a beautiful cabin up in the lakes and every afternoon her husband would take out the speedboat and we would all get on board and head out around the lake. I remember to this day being fascinated at the wake the small speedboat could leave behind. In that moment, I realised it's not how big or small we are in life that matters; it's the vibration we leave behind that creates the most lasting effect.

- Leaders relentlessly upgrade their teams, using every encounter as an opportunity to mentor, evaluate and build self-confidence.

- Encourage your staff to bring problems to you so that together you can turn them into solutions.

- Never neglect detail; when everyone's mind is distracted, the leader must be doubly vigilant.

- Organisations don't really accomplish anything; only by attracting the best people will you accomplish great deeds.

- Being responsible means you will sometimes annoy people. Keep going.

- Always have the courage to make unpopular decisions and trust your gut.

- Establish trust with candour, transparency and credit.

- Take risks and set an example. Urge your staff to try new things and live at the far edges of their comfort zones.

- Ask great questions, unleash debate and raise issues that get action.

- Go out and get under everyone's skin. Exude optimism and positive energy.

- Remember to celebrate; it helps to create an atmosphere of recognition and positivity.

Being yourself

There is something very special about being around someone who is genuine and happy in their own skin. You only have to play for a while with a small child to get in touch with what being yourself is all about. Outstanding leaders are easy to be around and they know first of all who and what they are before they lead anyone else.

■ Stop comparing yourself to others; learn to be content with yourself.

■ Be proud of yourself, not for how you look but for the content of your character.

■ Resist impulses to label yourself with descriptions that limit you. Statements such as 'I'm not good at...' will only serve to strengthen a limiting self-image. You can be good at anything if you choose to.

■ Ask yourself daily if you are dressing or behaving in ways that please you or to fit in. Once you're aware of your motivation you can choose how to behave – see how much better you feel.

■ Remember that nothing or nobody except you can make you unhappy unless you allow it.

■ Change the conversation in your head; stop the negative chatter. Imagine your head is a radio with two stations, negative FM and positive FM. Choose to switch and listen to positive FM each day.

Seconds to ponder ⏱

What does your presence say about you?

....

....

Who are you?

....

....

On a scale from 1 to 10, how great do people feel about themselves in your presence?

....

....

How visible are you currently as a leader?

....

....

In what three new ways could you increase your visibility?

....

....

Are you 100% happy in your own skin?

....

....

Where, in the past three months, have you let your ego get in the way of your presence?

....

....

How, in the past thirty days, have you let your team know you are there for them?

....

....

How have you made a difference to the business in the last six months?

....

....

What are the first impressions people get when they walk into your organisation?

....

....

On a scale from 1 to 10, how self-aware are you as an outstanding leader?

....

....

How many times in the last twenty-four hours have you complained?

....

....

Seconds to action ⏱

What actions will you take?

....

....

....

....

....

....

....

....

....

....

....

....

....

....

....

....

....

....

....

....

....

....

....

Seconds review

Six key lessons from chapter 1

1. Show up and be yourself.

2. Discover what you are here to do and dedicate your life to it.

3. Remember everywhere you go your presence leaves a resonance behind.

4. Your mind is a double mirror of your outer and inner worlds.

5. Live on your own terms not on those of someone else.

6. Presence has a radiance and inspires people with hope.

'Leaders of the future need to develop their inner as well as their outer capacity to deal with these complex times.'

Molly Harvey

Rituals

'Your daily rituals reflect your deepest values.'
Molly Harvey

All too often we look at outstanding leaders and assume they just got lucky or that they were born to lead. What we don't see is the discipline and some of the daily rituals that go into crafting the extraordinary impact they have and results they create. To be an outstanding leader takes work and very often leaders have to make sacrifices and pay the price in terms of dedication and self-control. They know and understand that leadership begins with their own self-leadership. They understand that daily rituals will keep them at their best and help them stay in a positive state.

To me a ritual is something that becomes part of your daily routine. In this chapter we will explore the many different rituals that I have come across in my work with corporate leaders.

The power of silence

Too many people around the world today live by the clock and the only quiet time they get is when they switch out the light to go to sleep. To me quiet time is thinking time; having the space and quietness to be creative leads to greater productivity in your life. Outstanding leaders build quiet time into their lives. For some people it is the early morning, while others prefer the evening.

I encourage you to practise being quiet even when everyone and everything around you is busy. I often enjoy the power of silence at busy airports or on train journeys. If you just have a great book to read the chaos going on around you will melt into the background.

- Set the clock half an hour earlier. Get up when the alarm goes and enjoy the early morning silence.

- Build daily quiet time into your diary.

- Sit quietly and take a mental vacation.

- When thoughts and issues flood your mind, observe them before letting them go.

- If a new idea goes through your head when in silence, make a note to write it down once you have finished.

- When you sit in silence, place a notebook and pen near you so that you can note any new ideas after your mental vacation.

- Explore different ways of experiencing silence, such as walking, meditating, yoga or simply sitting down. Once you've discovered what you most like, practise it regularly.

- Repeat your silence vacation every day at the same time for a minimum of thirty days.

- After thirty days it will become a daily ritual.

- If you miss your silence vacation one day, go back and start again at day one.

Dedicated learner

Outstanding leaders know that personal and professional greatness takes work. To be the very best in your field, become a passionate scholar of leadership. Earl Nightingale once said, 'If you spend one hour a day studying in your chosen field you will be a national expert in five years.' I became a dedicated learner in the field of human development at eighteen years of age and since then have continued to feed my curiosity about life and why I am here on the planet. Make time every day to feed your mind with great learning.

- When travelling take some books to read on the plane.

- Invest in an iPad or Kindle.

- Subscribe to great magazines.

- Dedicate some time every week to watching to some relevant YouTube videos.

- Watch TED lectures.

- Invest in CDs from Nightingale-Conant.

- Search for webinars and webcasts.

- Take notes and always review them afterwards.

- Start a book club.

- Become part of iLearning.

- Join abstract.com.

Personal energy

One thing I have noticed over the years that sets outstanding leaders apart is their level of fitness and energy. Physical good health helps us achieve all that we do and begins with what we put into our bodies. Before you eat something, get into the habit of asking yourself: 'Will this food make me feel tired?' 'Will this food make me feel light?'. Pay attention to your body and notice how it feels both minutes and hours after you eat something.

- Increase the quantity of green leafy vegetables you consume.

- Pay attention to your dietary balance between protein, carbohydrate and fat. See what works for your physiology and lifestyle.

- Start off each day with a glass of warm water and lemon, which helps to cleanse and detoxes your entire system. It also aids weight loss – try it for seven days and notice how much lighter you feel.

- Reduce your stress levels by finding the right exercise for you. Yoga and meditation are proven to reduce stress and increase the feeling of well-being.

- Multiple long-term studies have shown that those who exercise and enjoy an active lifestyle can expect more healthy years than their less active peers (one study averages about 3.5 extra years).

- Exercise two to three times per week to increase your mental clarity and energy, boost your heart health and stimulate your lymph flow.

Be responsible

Bill was the CEO of a large bank. I first worked beside him in 2006 as the company developed a state of the art leadership programme. His presence and leadership style fascinated me. One day while we were having lunch, I asked Bill if he would share one golden nugget about being a leader; his reply was, 'Be responsible and develop your own character, you cannot lead if you are pretending or not committed.'

- Responsible leadership starts with self-leadership.

- Be an advocate for what your business stands for.

- Create an ethical organisation.

- Trying to get everyone to like you is a sign of mediocrity that will lead you to avoid making tough decisions. Being responsible sometimes means you have to make the hard decisions.

Values driven organisation

Lynae Steinhagen from Madd-Steiny Productions believes that there is a strong relationship between values and outstanding leadership. Values inform actions and decisions. Leaders who are clearly in touch with their values lead with intention. They will lead with a sense of purpose that people pick up on and connect with. It is important for an employee's personal values to be in alignment with company values otherwise great talent will leave.

- Carry out a value assessment throughout the organisation to measure and correlate personal and organisational values.

- Ask employees to select the six values that best describe them.

- Ask employees to describe the top six values that represent how their culture operates.

- Ask employees to select the six values that represent for them a high performance organisation.

- Together, create company values that you and your people are proud of.

- Values serve as powerful guideposts to actions and attitudes.

- Make it a ritual to revisit the company values every six months and live by them every day.

Five people

You are the sum total of the five people you hang around with most of the time. I first heard that statement from Jack Canfield in 2003 at a convention in Arizona. Outstanding leaders never get together to talk about how bad things are; they choose not to be victims and choose to be around people who believe in possibility.

- Limit the amount of personal time you spend around negative people.

- Make a decision today to have at least five change-makers in your inner circle of friends.

- Outstanding leaders understand that the environment around them affects their results.

- Outstanding leaders think differently from average leaders.

- Your leadership consciousness will be the average of the five leaders you associate with.

- If the people currently around you are victims, change the people around you.

Honest conversations

One of the rituals that we implemented in our business many years ago was that at every meeting with consultants and work colleagues we would set aside ten minutes for an honest conversation slot. It has helped create a climate in which every team member understands that the leader wants to hear the bad news as well as the good. As a leader it is important that you create a climate in which people feel safe to share bad news so that a solution can be found quickly.

- Constantly encourage people to step forth and share what they perceive as bad news so it can be addressed in a timely manner.

- Ask the person who shared the news, 'What do you think?'. These are the four most important words to use when communicating effectively in any organisation.

- Encourage the team to work together to quickly and effectively find a solution to deal with the bad news.

Customer touch

Horst Schulze, a past president of the Ritz Carlton, was passionate about customer touch. Every time the company opened a new hotel he was part of the hiring process. When people came for interviews, the first thing he told them was what the Ritz Carlton stood for: 'We are ladies and gentlemen serving ladies and gentlemen.' The Ritz Carlton motto defines how the company values each employee as well as the service those employees provided to their customers. Horst was a demanding leader who set extremely high standards of excellence, quality and service and expected the Ritz Carlton to be regarded as the market leader in the hotel industry.

- Horst understood that his people would treat the customers the way they were treated.

- Horst wove values, respect, caring and trust into the very heart of the organisation.

- Horst passionately believed that helping the employee succeed was the key to customer service and business success.

- Take time to select the right people for roles and never hire someone just to fill a position.

- Know who your customers are – could you call them by name?

- Do your customers know who you are? If they saw you would they recognise you?

Celebrate success

Why does the word 'celebrate' make some leaders so nervous? The idea of throwing a party just doesn't seem professional; it often makes leaders worry that they won't look serious to the 'powers that be' above them or that maybe if people become too happy in the workplace they won't work so hard.

I passionately believe there is not enough celebration in the workplace any more.

- Celebration creates an atmosphere of recognition and positive energy.
- Work is too much a part of life not to recognise and mark moments of achievement.
- Create a hall of fame wall with photographs of outstanding employees.
- Establish a behind the scenes awards ceremony specifically for those whose actions are not usually in the limelight.
- Start an employee recognition programme. Give points for attendance, teamwork, punctuality, and so on and provide gift certificates for employees who reach certain goals.

Sweat the detail

Conrad Hilton, the owner of Hilton Hotels worldwide, was at a retirement party when someone asked him what the secret of success was. He said, 'Always remember to tuck the shower curtain into the bath tub.' Outstanding leaders pay attention to details.

- Even the greatest ideas and visions are worthless if they can't be implemented rapidly and efficiently.

- When other people's minds are dulled or distracted, outstanding leaders must be doubly vigilant and continually encourage their people to challenge the process.

- Do everything with excellence by making yourself a model of attention to detail.

- Encourage everyone around you to sweat the detail.

- Pay attention to what is going on around you.

- Continually step back, analyse and take stock.

- What is working?

- What do you need to stop?

- What do you need to implement?

Make family number one

On our leadership programme one of the first thing I ask participants to do is rate themselves, on a scale from 1 to 10, on their current leadership performance at work. Generally leaders find that question quite easy. My next question is always, 'On a scale from 1 to 10 how would you rate your leadership with family and friends?'. A question I regularly get thrown back at me is, 'What has leadership got to do with family?'

Leadership is about making an impact on the whole of your life, not just in the workplace. I know many great leaders who have sacrificed family and relationship time while climbing the corporate ladder, until one day everything crumbles around them. Balance is the key.

- Once you get home, greet your family members straight away. Don't switch on the TV, read the paper or turn your computer on.

- Put a one night a week date night with your partner in your diary.

- Celebrate every day; for example, get home for dinner when you can.

- Become involved in your children's interests.

- At the beginning of each new year, blank out your holiday time in your diary.

- Find moments in your day to stop and talk to your children. Treasure those moments.

- Leave your work at work or in your car before you enter your home.

- Create family values where you enjoy doing things together; for example, watching a film or having a takeaway.

- Learn to lean on each other and watch the trust and love build in the home.

Say no to distractions

Distractions rob us of time and energy. The more you become aware of what you are doing with your time, the more you will then be able to cut out distractions.

One very simple discipline that helps me overcome distractions is 'chunking' my time. To do this I divide my time in to sixty and ninety-minute chunks. Focus on one task and dedicate time to it. Strip away all distractions and simplify.

- Learn to ignore the small stuff.
- Turn off texts, tweets and your computer when focusing on large projects.
- Begin each day with a focused mind.
- Set aside exercise time in the middle of your day if possible; for example, walk around your office block.
- Allocate time slots when colleagues are welcome to interrupt you – make sure they know that at other times you should be left in peace.
- Set a time each day in which you will do your repetitive and boring tasks.
- Cut out long personal calls during the day.
- Limit your time on the internet.
- Plan mini-breaks within your day.

Forgive and let go

Forgiveness is a skill that many great leaders live by. Only by letting go of past baggage and failures can you truly move forward into the future.

Leadership is all about looking for the best in people and seeing through the eyes of understanding. Most of the mistakes that people make result from of a lack of awareness.

- Forgiveness does not mean that you condone bad behaviour or the actions of someone else; it just means you are making a choice to think differently about what happened.

- Forgiveness can take time; recognise that forgiveness is for you and not for anyone else.

- Forgiveness is a choice not an emotion.

- Remember when you carry resentment, the only person you are hurting is yourself.

- When you forgive another, you cut the ties and set yourself free.

- Keep it simple; forgive one thing at a time.

- Weigh your priorities; evaluate what is important in life.

- You will feel better, healthier and laugh more.

- You will reclaim your power and the right to run your own life.

Seconds to ponder ⏱

What current daily rituals do you have?

....

....

Which rituals are sabotaging your success?

....

....

How much thinking time do you build into your diary each week?

....

....

What are your six personal values?

....

....

Who are the five people you spend the most time with?

....

....

When did you last celebrate success?

....

....

What do you need to stop doing?

....

....

Where in business could you 'sweat the detail' more?

....

....

How much learning time have you currently built into your day?

....

....

Which current rituals increase your personal energy each day?

....

....

How many honest conversations have you had in the workplace in the last thrity days?

....

....

Seconds to action ⏱

What actions will you take?

....
....
....
....
....
....
....
....
....
....
....
....
....
....
....
....
....
....
....
....
....
....
....
....

Seconds review

Seven key lessons from chapter 2

1. Every day before you go out into the world, make time to be with yourself.

2. Build thinking time into your diary each week.

3. Stop being addicted to busyness.

4. Pay attention to your daily rituals – are they taking you in the direction you want to go?

5. Extraordinary results come from daily rituals done consistently.

6. Buy a gratitude journal and make a ritual of writing in it every day for at least five minutes.

7. Create an image of what you want in life and look at it every day.

'The daily rituals you do today are preparing and aligning you for the future you have yet to live.'

Molly Harvey

Discipline

'Discipline is the refining fire by which talent becomes ability.'
Molly Harvey

It takes discipline to be an outstanding leader. Discipline is all about the choices that you make every day. You give yourself a command and then you make the decision to follow through with it.

I made a decision on how I wanted to live my life many years ago at the National Speakers Association in Dallas. I came back from the USA knowing that I had to let go and say 'No' to others so that I could say 'Yes' to myself and focus on my life's purpose, which is to speak and to write. That also meant I had to be disciplined about the people who were around me.

I first met Jack Canfield in Arizona in 2003 and I will never forget when he asked me two very important questions. The first was, 'Who are the five people who are around you on a consistent basis?' and the second was, 'On a scale from 1 to 10 how positive are these people in your life?'. I realised in that moment that we become who we hang around with all day long.

Over the years I have noticed that when I am around great minds, my income and creativity go up but if people with a victim mentality are in my life my income goes down. I encourage you to walk away from that which you no longer want in your life. It is better to be in your own quiet company than bad company. Life is just one long moment so be disciplined about who your share your energy with.

Discipline brings about clarity of mind and helps you shut out distractions. It takes discipline to do the difficult things in life first. I once heard a great quote, 'To have what the very few have, do what the very few do.' To be stunningly magnificent at what you do in life takes focus, simplicity and the self-discipline to live your life on your own terms.

Discipline of managing your time

In today's fast-paced world, it is easy to lose perspective on what's important. Many years ago in one of Brian Tracey's books, I learned a golden nugget connected with managing your time. He recommended that before you do any task, you ask yourself the following question. Will this task take me closer to, or further away from where I need to be right now? One powerful question can help refocus your mind and your time.

- Say no to unscheduled activities; don't do them just because you thought of them.

- Say no to drop-in visitors.

- Only check your emails two or three times a day.

- Outstanding leaders are ruthless when it comes to controlling their time.

- Time and energy are two of your most special commodities; use them wisely.

- Shift from not valuing to valuing your time.

- If you know somebody efficient ask them what their secret is and how they developed their efficient habits. Then implement these habits in your life.

- Work in your real performance times.

Be more curious about life

When we are curious about life, we begin to think differently and dream more. Leaders know that many dreamers are also great visionaries who have left the safe harbour of the known.

■ Make a decision to learn something new every day.

■ Instead of asking, 'How can I *have* more?', ask yourself, 'How can I *be* more?'.

■ In your journal, write down a list of the top fifty things you are curious about in life. Then go out and learn more about them.

■ Use your curious mindset to look at your current high leverage activities.

■ Book twenty minutes of curiosity time into your diary each day and take time to see all the opportunities in the world.

■ Curiosity leads to clarity; clarity leads to action; action leads to results.

■ Curiosity about life is the number one mind food.

■ Being curious about your purpose in life helps you focus on what is important.

■ Curiosity has a simplicity to it. Embrace simplicity from today.

Be disciplined and improve your productivity

Productivity is all about taking action and getting things done. I learned many years ago to start my day by doing the difficult things first and breaking down the larger tasks into smaller chunks.

- Turn off all technology for at least ninety minutes each day and concentrate on your most difficult tasks.

- Chunk your 'to-do' list into ninety minute cycles; for example, ninety minutes of phone calls, ninety minutes to answer all emails.

- Don't check your emails first thing in the morning.

- Always have a large jug of water by your desk so you can keep hydrated as you work.

- When concentrating on a project, do not answer your phone every time it rings.

- When you work, be there and be fully engaged.

- Once a week on a Sunday, sit for ten minutes and write down what you want to do during the following week.

- Put space in your diary each week for thinking time, where you renew your mindset and refuel your energy.

Cut out useless meetings

These days one of the biggest wastes of time within organisations worldwide is too many meetings and not enough action. While working with leaders from a major retail company, a decision was made to cut out useless meetings.

At the beginning of each meeting, a timekeeper was chosen to keep people on track and make sure all the actions were achieved before the end of the meeting. Most meetings were cut down to thirty minute slots. Within a month, people were looking forward to attending short, precise and action-orientated meetings.

- Have meetings standing up.

- Make sure there is a start and end time to each meeting you attend.

- Ask yourself, 'On a scale from 1 to 10, how important is this meeting?'.

- Delegate the meeting to a member of your team.

- Make sure the agenda has meeting times assigned to each topic.

- Nominate a timekeeper at each meeting to keep the group to time.

- End every meeting with the GAT technique, with every action being given a reason, assigned to a person, and given a completion date. Short and to the point.

- Every day ask yourself whether you are being productive or merely active.

- Create an innovative environment; for example, round white tables and space so meetings can be more creative.

Take disciplined action

Disciplined action is all about having a plan, but then following through with the execution. Many people talk about taking action and never do it. Disciplined action is all about moving forward one step at a time.

Discipline is doing what you really don't want to do so you can do what you really do want to do. Very often in life, the areas we need to be disciplined in are the areas we don't like. One of those areas is taking disciplined action in life.

Elbert Hubbard once said, 'Parties who want milk should not seat themselves on a stool in the middle of the field and hope that the cow will back up to them.' We must take action when faced with tasks we do not like.

- Stop talking and just do it.
- Make a list of the tasks you don't like and do them first.
- Watch your thinking and interrupt your distractions by taking action.
- Master your emotions at the beginning of each day.
- Chunk down the large tasks that haunt you.
- If fear is stopping you from taking action, do it anyway.
- Remember the more action you take on different tasks, the easier they become.
- Just get into the mood of how great you will feel when you have taken action and completed the task.

Clean up your messes

Areas of our life where there are uncompleted projects or issues with people we have not dealt with very often hold us in the past and keep us from fully embracing the present.

Get a sheet of paper and a pen. On the left side of the page write down all the messes in your life and on the right side write the solutions; what you are going to do about the messes. Letting go and cleaning up your mess leaves your subconscious mind free to work on what matters right now.

- Make a list of how and what you procrastinate on.

- Make an appointment with yourself and begin clearing up your life.

- Clean up your living space and workspace.

- Complete or get rid of any unfinished projects on your desk.

- Deliver any undelivered communications.

- Clean out and organise your personal files.

- Return anything borrowed.

- Get a handle on your primary relationships so that you have agreements and ground rules which support you.

- Resolve any broken agreements or promises you have not kept.

Create a powerful brand

Many years ago I heard a wonderful saying, 'People buy people then they buy your products and services'. Everything you do or say is an expression of your brand. Leaders understand that it takes between six and eleven seconds to make an impact.

- First impressions count. What message are your clothes sending? Your hairstyle, the state of your footwear and how much perfume you wear all speak volumes even before you open your mouth.

- Think and talk like your customer. Know at least ten things about each of your customers.

- Learn how to read your customers and staff quickly.

- Always be one step ahead.

- When you don't know something, say so; say, 'I don't know but I'll find out.'

- When out at functions, mix and mingle rather than staying in one spot.

- Always ask open-ended questions.

- Mirror your customer's body language and be genuine.

- Always do what you say you are going to do and when you said you would do it.

Recharge

Some of the most outstanding leaders I know are disciplined about stepping back and recharging throughout the day. Tony Schwartz, president and CEO of the Energy Projects, advocates a work style based on a series of sprints rather than a marathon. He says that intermittently pushing ourselves, then stepping back and recharging builds strength and that without renewal, our physical, emotional, mental and spiritual energy declines.

- Take a power nap each day. Winston Churchill once said napping during the day was the only way he could cope with his responsibilities. It restores energy more effectively than drinking a cup of coffee.

- Add morning meditation into your life.

- At lunchtime, get up from your desk and go for a walk.

- Where possible use the stairs instead of the lift. Count walking down and up the stairs as a mini-recharge.

- Twice a day stop what you are doing and read for ten or fifteen minutes; recharge while you read.

- Work with your energy patterns; know your up time and down time.

Disciplines to live by

Practical disciplines are all about common sense. I recently heard a friend from the Republic of Ireland say, 'Common sense is all too uncommon today'. Sometimes it means we stop and come back to basics. If only we all did what we know we should do all the time, life would be a lot simpler.

- Don't hurry when success depends on accuracy.

- Don't form conclusions until you have all the facts.

- Don't believe something is impossible without trying it.

- Don't waste your time on trivial matters.

- Don't think that good intentions are an acceptable excuse for doing nothing.

- Don't forget that people need role models. Be one.

- Don't forget that people need to feel special. Compliment them.

- Don't forget that people need to be understood. Listen to them.

- Don't forget that obstacles can never steal your dreams without your permission.

Common discipline

It is so easy to say or write the word 'discipline', yet to live by it each day takes perseverance and willpower. Common discipline is the ability to take action regardless of your emotional state.

- Discipline is about repetition and continuing to do the right thing every day.

- Most people lack the discipline to implement the habits that make common sense, common practice.

- If you want to get the right things done, you have to define clearly what you want and why you want it.

- Each day ask yourself how you can get done the things that you have visualised.

- Common discipline is all about your daily and weekly habits.

- Discipline of action helps you have pride and creates excellence in what you do.

- The more you master rapid refocusing, the more you will add discipline to your life each day.

- People really don't fail; they just stop being disciplined in taking action.

Discipline in the workplace

Outstanding leaders will never ask someone to do what they are not willing to do themselves. To create discipline in the workplace, lead by example and set boundaries; then lead your people with consistency every day.

- If processes around you are not helping you and your team towards success, get rid of them.

- Wake up and realise there are no short cuts; discipline is everything.

- Stop using excuses like, 'That won't work; we tried it in the past'.

- Never let yourself off the hook by letting old patterns and behaviours get in the way.

- Build momentum every day by imagining that you are one step closer to completing your vision.

- Every month stop and look at your disciplines. Let go of what used to work and create new routines that work now.

- Remember that you are the problem and the solution.

- Know that there is no room for complacency.

- Get rid of your comfortable habits; they will only keep you stuck.

Commitment

Commitment is about saying and doing the things you said you would do long after the thoughts and feelings regarding what you said you would do have passed.

Commitment is not, I will do it when: ...I have time ...things change within the workplace. True commitment is taking action and moving forwards today.

- Develop a greater sense of self-awareness and encourage all your team to also become self-aware.

- Being world-class at anything in life first requires commitment.

- Develop a commitment charter and get your team to buy into it.

- Make a commitment to become excellent at what you do.

- Hold yourself and your team accountable for driving and sustaining excellence.

- Commit to being a life-long learner so you can continually increase your business acumen and personal and team effectiveness.

- Make a commitment to yourself never to back down when the going gets tough.

- Commitment is doing a job that no one else wants to do so that you can increase your learning.

Discipline of coaching

Leaders encourage everyone around them to step up and step forth in their lives by coaching them to the next level. I know I am where I am in my life because I am the product of the great coaches I have met along the way. Many of those coaches have encouraged me to see what I did not see in myself. Coaching unlocks the door to your creativity and the enormous potential within yourself.

- Stop trying to change people who feel they are in the wrong job within the company (round pegs won't ever fit in square holes).

- Stop trying to coach people who think everyone else is the problem. Wake up and smell the roses, it's impossible to fix people who think someone else is the problem.

- Be careful, you could be the problem.

- Realise we are all heroes in our own world; change begins and starts with you.

- The ideas you give to others are very often the ideas you need to implement yourself.

- People ignored take up far more time than people tended.

- Are you the coach you always wanted to be? If not, why not?

- Step back, listen and hear what everyone around you has to say.

- Every outstanding leader has a coach.

Believe in yourself 100%

Don't waste your time chasing and worrying if someone else believes in you. Leaders know that belief starts within themselves.

Many years ago Oprah Winfrey said some wise words I have never forgotten: 'You have to keep believing in yourself when everyone else around you doubts you.' That to me is believing in yourself 100%.

- Deal with your inner negative voice by imagining it is a little person. Now help it pack a suitcase and send it on a permanent holiday out of your life.

- Do a flip and turn all your weaknesses into positives.

- Create a powerful vision of yourself and *be* it every day.

- Always be prepared to go the extra mile and do whatever it takes to make a lasting difference in life.

- When others don't believe in you, stop, turn inwards and continue to believe in yourself.

- Look in the mirror every day for four weeks and say the words, 'I like myself'.

- Keep an achievements journal and in moments of doubt open it and read it.

- If you lack self-confidence, know that it is only a frame of mind and you can change it.

- Reframe how you see failure and struggle. See it as a positive life-changing part of your journey.

Seconds to ponder ⏱

Think of one goal you want to accomplish within the next three months to which you will apply discipline.

....

....

Think of one thing you will do differently in your life by applying discipline.

....

....

What will you change in your environment to help you be more disciplined?

....

....

What and who will you say 'No' to in life so you can practise the art of discipline?

....

....

What are the three daily disciplines that you will add to your life that will improve your productivity?

....

....

Name one comfortable habit you will let go of and be disciplined about.

....

....

Think of one new habit in which you could manage your time more effectively.

....

....

How many times per day do you check emails?

....

....

What meetings could you cut out of your diary in the next two weeks?

....

....

How will you recharge within the next twenty-four hours?

....

....

What one commitment will you follow through in the next seven days?

....

....

Seconds to action ⏱

What actions will you take?

....

....

....

....

....

....

....

....

....

....

....

....

....

....

....

....

....

....

....

....

....

....

....

Seconds review

Seven key lessons from chapter 3

1. Be disciplined about who you spend your time with.

2. Discipline takes persistence and the courage to say, 'No'.

3. Discipline is doing something even if you don't feel like it.

4. Clean up your messes with discipline.

5. The most important disciplines in your life are never comfortable.

6. Simplicity requires ruthlessness and discipline.

7. Be disciplined and ask yourself each day, 'If this is the only thing I accomplish today, will I be satisfied?'

'Discipline is all about taking action on those projects you don't feel like doing now, so that tomorrow you can look back in relief and say it's done and I did it.'

Molly Harvey

Trust the inner satnav

'It is the soul's duty to be loyal to its own desires; it must abandon itself to its master passion.'
Dame Rebecca West

To trust our inner satnav we have to think and live from the inside out. It is as if we have to go back to being a child again. You have to trust that small, quiet guidance system within you completely. The only thing standing between you and your inner guidance system is your mind. Your guidance system will never let you down and sometimes it speaks to us in dreams, books or through other people.

Trust your bad feelings; they can be a warning of danger ahead, just as your car's navigation system warns you that you are driving over the speed limit. I was recently at dinner with a business associate and she told me that Sir Richard Branson knows within sixty seconds of meeting a new person and shaking his hand if he would make a good business partner or not. He currently has over 300 companies under the Virgin brand. Throughout history, all the great wisdom keepers of the world have used some form of intuition.

I realise now that from a very young age my inner guidance system was gently moving and shaping my life's purpose. I can remember being seven years old and playing by myself around a huge oak tree in a big field on the country estate where I grew up and something inside me said, 'pretend the field is full of thousands of people and talk to them.' Now I know I was being prepared for what I currently do around the world.

Few of us have any training on how to turn inwards and yet most of the outstanding leaders I have met over the years are people who have developed their intuition and learned to trust their gut feelings. Everyone has intuition; it's just a matter of developing it. Make time every day to listen to yours.

Your intuition can provide you with answers to anything you need to know. Ask questions beginning with 'what' or 'should I'. Write down your answers and take immediate action. I call that type of activity 'inspired action' and I find it is very rarely wrong.

Innovation

Outstanding leaders very often facilitate the innovation process by asking provocative and challenging questions of everyone around them. They ask questions like 'what if?', 'why not?' and 'why?' Innovation is really a mindset and involves creating the right environment around you and your people.

- Have a vision for change and communicate it every day.

- Break all the rules and challenge every assumption. Business is an art; create new ways to satisfy the customer every day.

- Welcome failure so that you can learn more quickly.

- Identify the mavericks within your team and harness their ideas.

- Give people space and time to be innovative.

- Give up needing to be the smartest person in the company.

- When you delegate, delegate and let go.

- Reward people who disagree with you.

- Look behind wild ideas for potential new direction.

- Get rid of fear from the workplace and foster excitement.

Inner wisdom

Leadership is about living and working from the inside out. Leadership is not simply something you do every day; it is something that comes from inside you. Do your actions each day come from a place deep within you or are they coming from a shallower place? Only you can answer that question.

- To live from your inner wisdom takes repetition.

- Make a decision today to grow in wisdom as a leader.

- Let your decisions become more important than circumstances or desires for the moment.

- Seek out wise people who can help you grow.

- Find time each day to learn and study. Read the autobiographies of great leaders past and present.

- Keep yourself updated about what's happening, both the global perspective and in your own field.

- Always be open to learning something from everyone you meet.

Build trust

Trust starts with you; be consistent in your behaviour. Encourage people in the workplace to have honest conversations. Live your values and the company's values each day. Admit mistakes and take the blame. Develop a fear-free culture by spending time each day listening to your people.

- Never over promise.
- Never betray confidential information.
- Admit mistakes straight away.
- Acknowledge when you don't know something.
- Be responsive; respond to emails and phone calls quickly.
- Be personable; let your personality shine through.
- Be explicit and direct.
- Consider all employees as equal partners.
- Get rid of command and control and encourage learning from failure.

Inner drive

Inner drive to me means self-determination, and as leaders you have to believe fully in your vision for the future when, at first, maybe not everyone will be on board with you.

- Stop seeking drive outside yourself and know that it lives inside of you.

- Banish your ego; ego encourages you to stop learning.

- Inner drive is what will kick you out of bed in the morning and make you take action today.

- Listen to your inner drive and make a list of what it is telling you to do, then tape the list and listen to it every day.

- Before saying yes to a new project, stop and check that it is in alignment with your inner drive.

- Creativity and innovation will feed your inner drive.

- When you align with your inner drive, the gift and blessing of who you are and what you are here to do becomes clearer.

Heart energy

Outstanding leaders know that it takes real leadership to engage the hearts and minds of everyone they work with. As Robin Sharma says, 'People will not lend you a hand until you first touch their hearts'.

- Say 'thank you' a minimum of twelve times per day.

- Practise decency every day, and not just in the workplace.

- Let other people be right from time to time; it helps foster respect and mutual admiration.

- Know that people have a need to be valued, respected, listened to and involved.

- Where right now in business does your heartbeat flutter?

- Leading from the heart requires compassion and empathy.

- When you are with people, be there and feel the sense of connectivity.

- Learn to get out of your head and think with your heart.

- Heart leadership is all about speaking the truth and keeping people informed.

Trust your gut feelings

'Trust your gut'. We have all heard those three simple words. When we say them we mean listen to your intuition. Leaders know that sound intuition is built on years of experience, but I know many people who have great intuition and still they don't trust themselves.

- First impressions do count. If something doesn't feel right and you don't like someone, there is probably a reason for it.

- When considering a partnership, if your gut is telling you to run in the opposite direction and not sign the contract, trust it and don't sign the contract.

- Having strong intuition can give you a great head start when it comes to business meetings. Be aware of other people's feelings and body language.

- Start listening to your own feelings. Recognise the way your mind and body respond to gut feelings.

- When you learn to trust your gut feelings you will also be more emotionally intelligent and therefore able to develop better rapport with everyone you meet.

- Intuition is all about listening and following your attention and targeting what you can do.

- Intuition travels in time and space; it is instant.

- Trust your own inner information.

- Intuition works best when you apply it to logic and fact.

- Pay attention to the signs of what is happening around you in your life.

Simplicity

Leadership is about being able to simplify constantly. Every leader needs to explain clearly the top three things the organisation is working on. If you can't, you are not leading well. Leaders consistently work at making simple something that is complex.

- If you can't describe the strategy of your business in ten minutes, you haven't got a plan.

- Take short breaks frequently within your work day.

- Establish simple processes, establish routines, and assign tasks to the strengths of each team member.

- Choose quality over quantity.

- Never read or answer emails at the weekend.

- Set limits on everything; too much of anything can cause chaos.

- Focus on what is important, delete or delegate the rest.

- Create a joyful atmosphere wherever you go.

- Simplify the organisational structure. Reduce the level of layers.

- Prune and simplify products and services.

Thinking time

In my speaking keynotes I always talk about thinking time. I passionately believe that the number one reason a lot of businesses fail today is they don't take thinking time to be creative and innovative.

- Build in ninety minutes of creative thinking time in your day.

- Buy a journal and label it your 'Thinking Journal'.

- Switch off the car radio and have a recorder so you can capture your new ideas.

- For each ninety minute session, have a theme to your thinking time.

- Get out in nature; bring a pen and paper and write down your creative thoughts.

- Write down numbers 1 to 33 on a piece of paper. By each number put a new idea for your business.

- Break your new ideas into easy actions.

- Stop thinking of time as an unlimited commodity.

- Let your mind wander and daydream for ten minutes a day then write your thoughts in your journal.

Stay grounded

Too often in life when we climb the ladder of success we forget our roots and why we are doing what we do. That is why it is important to have a work-life balance and spend time with people you love and appreciate outside work.

I was back in Ireland recently and a friend of my mother's commented on how grounded I still was and that I had never lost the Irish accent. My reply was, 'why would I? That's why I come home so often.'

- Learn to work hard and play hard.
- Never lose touch with what matters in life, for example family and friends.
- Never lose touch with customers and employees.
- Create a small inner circle of trusted advisors around you.
- Ask only the people you totally trust for feedback.
- Dream big, yet every day do the small things that will help you stay grounded.
- Ask yourself every day, 'What do I stand for? What do I care about?'
- Surround yourself with people who inspire you.
- Be a humble learner.

Inspiration

Inspiration is about finding something that is inspiring and taking action on it. When leaders take inspired action they motivate everyone around them. Inspiration is the very thing that helps leaders create visionary companies.

- Never force people to follow you, invite them to walk with you.

- Truly inspirational leaders produce more leaders than followers.

- Notice the little things every day and say 'thank you'.

- Ask 'why not?' rather than 'why?'.

- Tap into the courage inside of you and be different.

- Practise tough empathy with your employees; care deeply about them yet never accept anything but the best.

- Always use language that is consistent with your actions.

- Surround yourself with what inspires you.

- Inspiration is a quality and a state of being.

Manage your ego

It is important to manage your ego otherwise it could become toxic.
An abundance of ego can get in the way of good leadership. If you have
to have the last word on everything be careful it doesn't affect your
staff's morale. The best way to approach leadership is a balance of self-
confidence and humility.

- Stop needing approval from others.

- Get over yourself and ask for help now and again.

- It is OK to be vulnerable at times; it shows you are fully alive and fully
  human.

- Stop comparing yourself to others. There will always be someone who
  is better or worse than you are.

- How much is enough? Greed is a function of ego.

- Understand that a certain amount of ego is healthy; it is what gets us
  out of bed in the morning.

- Remember there is a fine line between self-confidence and arrogance.
  Ego has hollowness in it.

- Let go of competition in your life and embrace creativity.

Creativity

Creativity is an essential leadership skill and it can be learned, but you have to make time and take time to be creative. Each time you find an easier and smarter way of doing things, you are being a creative leader.

- Every time you go to a meeting sit next to someone different.
- Move your office around twice a year.
- Add colour to your environment.
- Break your routine; instead of driving to work take the train or the bus.
- Study something new, read books on art, music or fantasy.
- Creativity is a muscle, exercise it every day.
- Never tell yourself you are not creative.
- Spend time with small children and watch them play.
- Listen to music and let your creativity flow.

Develop a listening ear

Leaders who communicate effectively have developed the listening ear. They not only listen to people but *hear* what they are saying. Many years ago I learned to develop the listening ear when I worked with an amazing priest called Fr. Jimmy O'Connell. He worked relentlessly to prepare and train young people to be leaders. He believed people were generally good listeners but not everyone heard what others were saying because too often we are too busy thinking how to reply.

- Leadership is about not only listening but also making a decision to make the time to hear what someone has to say without judgement.

- Develop a positive attitude towards listening.

- Learn to be others-focused rather than self-focused.

- Stop hijacking conversations while the other person is still talking.

- Remember we have two ears and one mouth...Shut Up!

- Always follow up after listening to conversations.

- Don't multi-task when someone is speaking to you.

- Listen with your heart, not just your ears.

- Ask questions and give people time to answer.

- Do you hear what people say or do you hear what you think they say?

Seconds to ponder ⏱

List two situations in the past where you have trusted your inner guidance system and it was right.

....

....

What time of the day will you take time out to listen to your intuition?

....

....

How has your mind in the past got in the way of your intuition?

....

....

Where in the past have you not trusted your gut only to find it was right all along?

....

....

How does your inner guidance system communicate with you?

....

....

What actions have you taken in the past as a result of listening to your intuition?

....

....

Who are the mavericks within your team?

....

....

Which systems could you simplify within the workplace?

....

....

How much thinking time have you currently booked in your diary?

....

....

Which practical habits help you to stay grounded every day?

....

....

On a scale from 1 to 10 how creative are you currently within the workplace?

....

....

List two things could you do within the next ninety days to encourage more creativity within the workplace?

....

....

Seconds to action ⏱

What actions will you take?

....

....

....

....

....

....

....

....

....

....

....

....

....

....

....

....

....

....

....

....

....

....

....

....

....

Seconds review

Seven key lessons from chapter four

1. Learn to turn inwards instead of outwards for all the answers you want in life.

2. Through the daily discipline of meditation be still and listen to your intuition.

3. Trust your intuition and take immediate action.

4. Pay attention to all the different ways your intuition speaks to you. For example: dreams, hunch, voice, gut feeling and emotions.

5. Invest in a journal and write down all your questions and answers.

6. Read books and invest in a course on business intuition.

7. Use crossword puzzles and lateral thinking exercises to develop your right brain.

'Outstanding leaders move forward in life by aligning their inner navigation systems with the outside world.'

Molly Harvey

Collaboration

'The key to leadership is connecting to and with the people you lead.'
William Arthur Ward

It has to start from the top. Unless the leaders of an organisation connect and collaborate effectively, culture change programmes are a waste of time and money. Too often culture change programmes are delegated to management while the top leaders stay in their ivory towers and wonder afterwards why the programme didn't work. Culture change and collaboration is an outcome not a process and it has to come from the top.

Why is it sometimes as if we are from different planets? People can be confusing and relationships difficult to understand. Very often instead of collaborating with others we compete and try to influence or persuade people and it doesn't always work. Over the last twenty-five years of working with organisations and their people I have come to realise that the difference between people is not minor, it's dramatic, and when we understand that we can collaborate much more effectively.

As I work throughout the world I hear rumblings within organisations. People are no longer willing to stay in organisations where they are made to feel under-valued or ill-informed. They want to work with leaders who are authentic, who will allow them to fulfil their potential and not ignore their emotional and spiritual sides. Outstanding leaders let their insides become their outsides. People will follow those leaders in times of change and will not follow leaders who don't ring true. More than ever before leaders are called upon to be the people they truly are and build a web of connections within and outside their organisations.

People grow in organisations where honesty is valued and where honesty is rewarded.

The new corporate leader has a holy man's compassion, a warrior's heart and the courage and authenticity to say no to anything that diminishes their own spirit or that of their people.

Collaborate when faced with conflict

Leaders use collaboration skills when faced with conflict. They realise that differences need not be a battleground; they can be a strength. Something magical happens when we collaborate. We move from communicating to connecting heart-to-heart, mind to mind, allowing us to celebrate our differences.

- Take control of the situation, not the person.

- Deal with difficult situations before they become disasters.

- Work co-operatively towards solutions.

- Always leave someone with the feeling that you are helping not reprimanding her.

- Speak only about how you want things to be rather than dwelling on the past. Talk the language of solutions rather than problems.

- Avoid any hint of blame, judgement or criticism.

- Talk about what you observe and see rather than what you think or believe.

- Feedback on the behaviours not the person.

- Use 'I' language by talking about your truth rather than implying you have the truth; that way you are less likely to appear accusatory.

- The way I see it...

- My perception is...

- Remember conflict not only has a high personal cost, but it is also expensive to the organisation.

- Build a climate within the organisation where people feel they can give feedback easily.

- Collaborate when faced with conflict; build bridges rather than barriers.

Understand people

To understand people fully the starting point must always be the other person. Outstanding leaders learn to ask great questions and then listen. Too often today we ask people questions and then hijack the conversation when we get a reply. Understanding people is one of the greatest skills needed to lead an organisation.

- Always make the other person your starting point.

- When we understand why people behave as they do we make better observations.

- People who are interested in others are themselves more interesting.

- When people feel good about the company they work for they produce more.

- To understand people more, stop complaining and learn to appreciate.

- Walk through your organisation with the eyes of a customer. View your people and departments as if it was the first time.

- Be sensitive to other people's needs within your team.

- The best way to inspire people to superior performance is to convince them by everything you do.

- Never assume that the other person's values are the same as yours.

- The most significant journey of your life is to meet someone halfway.

- Know the natural talents of your employees.

- Know their weaknesses as well.

Pay it forward

Paying it forward is all about doing something for someone else and not expecting anything in return.

In September 2008 sixty-five percent of my business fell away with the banking crash. A fellow speaker and friend, Clive Gott, started recommending my work to all his clients. It wasn't until after his sudden death in February 2011 that I found out that his favourite movie was *Pay It Forward* with Kevin Spacey and Helen Hunt. I watched it and realised that some favours you are not allowed to pay back. Where can you pay it forward for someone else today and expect nothing in return?

- People need role models, be one.
- People need to be understood, listen to them.
- People need to feel special, compliment them.
- People are often insecure, encourage them to be confident.
- Make it a habit to praise someone at least once per day.
- Say 'thank you' more often.
- Challenge staff and encourage them to go the extra mile.
- Recognise progress and effort.
- Send out at least three thank you cards per week.
- Send a text of thanks to at least three people who have made a difference in your life today.
- Write down the things you are grateful for right now in your life.
- Have fun prizes for your teams, for example a Pizza Party or an iPhone.

Achieve likeability as a leader

When you like someone you are far more open to listening to their ideas and suggestions. Likeability is not soft. I know many likeable leaders who make tough decisions every day in business and consistently achieve great results.

Every day within the workplace and your life in general, smile more. A sincere smile, not a fake smile.

- Likeability is much more important than superiority.
- Make eye contact when you shake someone's hands.
- Hold the handshake for no longer than two to three seconds.
- Outstanding leaders have a way of using simple words.
- Say what you have to say; keep it to the point.
- Don't impose your values on others; instead let your presence and your actions say what they are.
- When collaborating with others, find shared passions.
- Be natural, be yourself. There will never be another you.
- Likeable people create win-win situations.

Create trust

An environment of trust can be built only when leaders set the example.

Trust is all about perceived care and integrity and these values need to be demonstrated in every interaction. As human beings we all make mistakes every day. When you don't do the right thing admit it; be transparent, authentic and willing to share your faults. When you have nothing to hide you radiate trust.

- Conduct a trust audit throughout your organisation; it will allow you to gauge the current level of trust and identify a plan of action.

- Stop the game-playing that very often goes on behind the scenes of everyday interactions.

- Always act with honesty.

- Don't make promises if you cannot keep them.

- Make it a daily practice to pause and listen to other people's ideas.

- Trust develops from allowing people to make mistakes and take responsibility.

Empowering questions

When we ask empowering questions we instantly establish rapport and create a feeling of connection with another person. It also helps us to stop giving advice and let the other person come to their own conclusion.

- Create a culture that embraces questions, for example, 'what one idea/strategy are we not implementing in the business that could improve it?'

- Do not ask questions that will disempower your team, for example, 'why are you behind schedule?'

- To collaborate more effectively through a questioning approach make sure your communication does not come across as a telling approach.

- The better your questioning approach is the more information you will gain. You will also engage others and remove defensiveness.

- The purpose of good questions is to uncover hidden concerns.

- Use pace and silence effectively when collaborating.

- By asking the right questions leaders can uncover the fears, wants and interests of others and achieve better communication skills.

Make their day

Small gestures can have a big impact, for example, saying good morning and smiling when you get into the office. It helps create the feel-good factor within the workplace.

- Never walk around the office with your head down. Think what messages you are giving out to employees.

- Watch your use of words when communicating. Use simple, powerful words.

- When you arrive at work each day go out of your way to say good morning to as many employees as possible.

- Get into the habit of getting away from your desk during the day to meet people.

- Why not hold a breakfast session once a month and get to know employees at a deeper level?

- Eat in the company canteen. Every so often sit with employees and find out how happy they really are working for the company.

- Act on some of the suggestions employees give.

- Be consistent in what you say and how you behave.

- Be careful in meetings that you don't come across as having favourites while excluding others. Watch your body language; it never lies.

Never leave anyone behind

Leadership is all about not leaving anyone behind and that means being aware if someone is struggling within the team. By developing and creating a culture where honesty and openness can thrive, people will feel they can ask for help if they're struggling.

- Refuse to blame others.

- Suspend judgement when listening to others.

- Put yourself in other people's shoes.

- Let your team find the answer even if it is already clear to you.

- Create an environment where motivation can thrive.

- Give credit where credit is due.

- Never underestimate the ability of your team.

- Keep your eyes on future results; make sure all of your team is on board.

- Inspire, coach and empower.

Cut out bickering

Bickering within teams wastes time and energy. One way to handle the situation is to have a five minute session at the start of a meeting during which people can speak about what is annoying them or what they are unhappy about. Then spend a further ten minutes encouraging them to find solutions. Watch how the group reframes the situation.

- Take 100% responsibility for every decision you make.

- Give yourself permission to change your mind.

- Do not rush decision making; don't prolong it unnecessarily either.

- Stop, pause and reflect before you make a decision.

- Empower everyone around you with your decision.

- Cut out the bickering. Be clear with yourself and others involved about the steps you will take to reach the decision.

- Make sure you are in a positive frame of mind.

- Listen to your gut.

- Don't overanalyse.

Retain top talent

Keeping top talent consistently engaged can be a challenge. That is why you encourage your best people to get involved in difficult tasks so that they can constantly explore new and innovative ways to take the company forward.

- Make sure your people are engaged, not exhausted, every day at work.
- Cross train employees to do more and different jobs.
- Bring in recognition programmes to the workplace.
- If employees are leaving the organisation, find out why and address the issue quickly.
- Create a comfortable and inspirational environment.
- Have a great retention strategy in place.
- Create a culture where employees are allowed to speak their minds freely.
- Take time to meet new employees and learn about their talents, abilities and skills.
- As a leader make sure you encourage employees to have a work-life balance.

Thank you notes

Many years ago the great American psychologist William James said, 'the deepest human need is the need to be appreciated.' I recently received a telephone call from a university for which I'd done work about two years previously. The lecturer couldn't get to the management school because his car had broken down and the school asked if I could step in to do the afternoon lecture to thirty entrepreneurs. When I got to the university the administration manager thanked me for sending them a thank you card when I'd last worked for them. She had put the card up on the cork board of the office and inside was my telephone number.

- One of my weekly rituals has been to sit down and write thank you cards to people who touch my life.

- Never overlook the simple act of sending a thank you card.

- Writing a thank you card or note is a great opportunity to let someone know you care. All it requires is your time.

- The thank you cards that people love the most are handwritten.

- A thank you card sent to customers humanises you and your company.

Shut up

From a very early age I learned the discipline of shutting up. I realised that if I kept quiet the other person would always fill the silence. Everyone has a story to tell if only we could learn to pause after asking a question. It takes patience to wait and allow embarrassing silence to fill the conversation.

- When we pause and stay quiet we develop the skill of being strategic listeners and that is an important skill for all leaders.

- When you ask a question practise pausing and shutting up.

- Practise strategic listening by asking great questions.

- Learn to be comfortable with the silent spaces in conversations when you collaborate with another.

- Remember, if you are quiet for long enough the other person will probably find the answers to the questions themselves.

Culture of personal growth

Outstanding leaders understand that the company can only grow as fast as its people do, and they back that up with job training to encourage a culture of personal growth.

At one company I know, Defender Direct (maker of security systems in Indianapolis), the President Marcia Rabb sets aside two hours each Monday for new employees to talk about goal setting and how each of them can get the best results by using their top three strengths. Throughout the employees' careers they attend different life programmes all paid for by the company. All this is not a touchy feely business. Marcia knows that the company is world-class at what it does and it continues to exceed its profit targets year after year.

- Continually build and develop a strong sense of engagement among your teams.

- Bring in speakers for regular lunch and learn sessions.

- Start a book club with a reading list of suggested titles that underscore your company's values.

- Develop an off-site development programme to help all employees to identify their strengths.

- Encourage staff to start office based activities such as sport, green or volunteer initiatives.

Future framers

Bob Danzig went from office boy to CEO of Hearst Newspapers, overseeing its 6,000 workers. He was so respected as a leader that he led Hearst for two decades. Growing up he never had a family and spent his early years living in foster homes. As he went to his fifth foster home, his social worker said three words to him that transformed his life: 'You are worthwhile.'

- Bob called all the new talent that joined the company 'Future Framers'.

- He passionately believed companies were simply a place to gather talent.

- He believed the level of your willingness as a leader is directly correlated to the level of success you are going to achieve in business.

- Watch your words; they have a resonance in the minds of everyone whose lives you touch.

Kindness

Many of us believe that in order to live a truly successful life we must achieve some grand feat that will put us on the front cover of magazines. Nothing could be further from the truth; a meaningful life is made up of small acts of kindness that over time add up to something truly amazing. I learned about the wisdom of kindness from a great mentor in Minnesota, Louise Griffiths. Her wise words were, 'You can always choose kindness and it doesn't cost anything.'

- Leaders know that finding good people and treating them well is the key to business growth.

- Nine out of ten people are more productive when working around nice people.

- Compliment a work colleague on their excellent work.

- Buy an inspirational book for a friend.

- Smile a lot.

- Every day make the business world a kinder place.

- Kindness is not soft; kindness has a bottom line effect.

- People will always remember the quality of their human interaction with you.

- Be grateful for where you are in your life. Where you are now is not where you are going, be grateful for the now.

Seconds to ponder ⏱

On a scale of 1 to 10 how well do you connect and collaborate with everyone you meet?

....

....

What actions can you take right now to improve your communication skills?

....

....

What is the core leadership message that you communicate every day?

....

....

In what way does the team need you?

....

....

How do you currently communicate your message in a clear concise way?

....

....

What are the top three strategies of the members in your team?

....

....

How are you maximising them each day?

....

....

Write down three names of people who you will collaborate with within the next seven days?

....

....

What one thing have you done in the last ninety days to improve and maintain the level of trust in the organisation?

....

....

How many personal growth programmes are available to staff each year?

....

....

How many thank you notes have you sent in the last thirty days?

....

....

How many conversations have you hijacked within the last twenty-four hours?

....

....

Seconds to action ⏱

What actions will you take?

....

....

....

....

....

....

....

....

....

....

....

....

....

....

....

....

....

....

....

....

....

....

Seconds review

Seven key lessons from chapter four

1. Always remember that people are assets not liabilities.

2. Always make the other person your starting point.

3. People don't care how much you know about them once they realise how much you care about them.

4. Trust is the bedrock upon which all meaningful collaborations are built.

5. Practise listening twice as much as you talk.

6. Never assume that someone else's values are the same as yours.

7. Connecting and collaborating with people should come naturally; it must never be forced or fake.

'Collaboration happens when two or more people get together and share their collective spark, heart-to-heart, mind-to-mind.'

Molly Harvey

⑥ Focused action

'An ounce of action is worth a ton of theory.'
Friedrich Engels

People often ask me how it is that I seem to get so much done and achieve so much. My reply is always the same, 'stop talking and take action'. The world doesn't pay you for what you know; it pays you for what you do.

Outstanding leaders keep taking action each day.

Each morning I open my diary and look at my 'to-do' list. I start at number one and work down through the list. Over the years I have developed the focus to cut out distractions and focus on the task. I now batch my tasks into ninety-minute pockets, taking a break between each task.

To me focused action is all about the bigger vision; once you know what that vision is do two to three things that align with it every day. The hardest step is always the first step. Once you've taken it keep walking in that direction, remembering to never, ever give up. Once you take action the 'how' and 'what' will fit into place.

I live my life by the eighty per cent rule. Once I am eighty per cent there I start taking massive action, learning along the way.

Most people spend their whole life talking and preparing to take action. Why not make your 'some day' today and quit waiting, quit worrying about 'what if' and do it now?

Focused action is also about inspired action, it is as if something inside of you is saying 'do it'. You were born to be more and do more.

I came to live in England in October 1998 with £500 in my pocket and a head full of dreams. I got a job within thirteen days of arriving and soon came across a magazine by Nightingale Conant. As I looked at the magazine, something inside of me said, 'one day you will be in this magazine.' I remember laughing to myself and thinking that I'm not American and I don't know the right contacts. Over the next twenty-three years I held onto the dream and purchased many tapes and CDs. Then in 2010 I wrote to the Director of Nightingale Conant, including some of my CDs and one of my books. One afternoon in November I got a call from their marketing department saying they would like to feature my work in their 2011 catalogue. In that moment I realised it is never too late to take action.

Take focused action

Focused action is all about being more active. Successful leaders prepare, set a plan and then work to the plan rather than waiting for something to happen some day. Why not make your some day this day?

I recently watched a video of Richard Branson being interviewed about why he felt he was a success. One of the comments he made was that he rarely worked in an office environment; he got a lot of his work done from his home office in England or Necker Island. He spoke about the discipline of focus; writing a plan then taking action on that plan by cutting out distractions.

- Start each day with a plan.
- Shut out distractions; don't turn on email, Facebook, Twitter or any other social media sites.
- Start with a clutter-free desk.
- Use a timer. Set it to give you ninety minute chunks of focus.
- Work within your peak energy times.
- After ninety minutes take a refreshing break.
- Work from a location other than your desk, maybe from home, the library or a book store.
- Find a buddy who will hold you accountable and who would also like to improve her own focus.

Visualise and be it now

Leaders visualise the future on the inside before developing it on the outside. Every morning, make time to sit down and visualise your day ahead. One of my favourite sayings is, 'be there before you get there'.

- Leaders always think about the future and how to get to the goals that they set.

- Let the past go. Be in the present and walk into the future you want by visualising it every day.

- Create an environment around you that prepares you for the future.

- Shoot for the stars; write in your journal what your future will look like in five, ten and fifteen years from now.

- Visualise and meditate on your goals daily.

- Mastermind with other leaders.

- Know what gives you energy, what takes your energy and what wastes your time.

- At the end of the day just before you pop off to sleep, visualise the next day and see it all unfolding as you want it to.

- Look at what everyone else is doing and visualise something different.

Talk less

Leadership is more about taking action than talking. Everything changes when we take action. Leaders know they are paid to be scared and push through adversity. What are the important decisions you need to make today so that every day you can take action and manage those decisions?

- For one week ask more questions; watch what is going on around you, talk less and take more action.

- At your next meeting experiment by asking more questions rather than making statements.

- If you have too many projects on the go, clear them all and start from scratch.

- Take a day off and notice how you will come back ready to take action.

- When you say you will do something, do it.

- Be accountable to yourself.

- Remove the word 'should' from your language and add the word 'choice' instead.

- Continually develop your self image and watch how much more action you take in life.

Determination

Determination is all about never giving up, overcoming setbacks and pushing through to the next step. Determination challenges your assumptions, overcoming what scares you and disrupting your old patterns.

- The difference between what's not possible and what is possible is your level of determination.
- Outstanding leaders are ordinary people with extraordinary determination.
- Great leaders continue to re-invent themselves through determination.
- Know that there is a thin line between determination and obsession; balance is the key.
- Determination is the commitment to keep going when everyone laughs at you.
- Determination is that inner knowledge that you will succeed one day.
- Determination is a state of mind that you build day by day.

See all problems as challenges

It takes discipline to reframe problems as challenges and turn them into opportunities. When we train our minds to look for the lesson in every problem it helps us to solve the challenge and move forward in our lives more quickly.

- Train yourself to see every problem as a challenge so that you can overcome it.

- Ask for help and admit it quickly if you have made a mistake.

- Practise patience and perseverance.

- The days of micromanagement are over. Inspire everyone around you to seek solutions.

- Keep learning, keep growing, and never stop.

- Get out of the way, let go of control and trust others.

- Listen, engage and then share your opinion.

- View change as a challenge and foster hardiness.

- Ask yourself how important this issue will be one month from now and you will give yourself a great reality check.

Passion

Passion is that positive flame inside each and every one of us that starts from the inside and radiates out. Passion is contagious. When we are passionate about what we do in life it eases everything we do and say. I made a decision many years ago that I never want to retire. Why? Because I have found what I am here to do and it never feels like work. Each day is another chance to be passionate and go out and make a difference in life.

- Be knowledgeable; try to know everything that is going on in your field of business.

- Every day sharpen the leadership skills that will continue to give you the edge.

- Trust and follow your heart energy as well as your head energy.

- Every day raise the bar of your integrity and your level of personal mastery.

- Find the fun in what you do and treat your employees and everyone you're surrounded by in a heartfelt attentive way.

- You need both passion and compassion to lead.

- Every day share what you know with others.

- Every day inspire yourself and others to action.

- Know who you truly are and be consistent in your decisions and behaviour.

Storyboard your vision

Storyboards are a representation of what you want to happen in your life. When I was young I didn't have my own bedroom until I was eight years old when my mum and dad had a large bathroom extension added to the house. The new bathroom was so large that half the room became my bedroom. I can still remember those white walls that became my first storyboard. You are never too young or too old to start storyboarding. Walt Disney created the Disney empire through storyboarding.

■ Brainstorm and write down what you want to achieve in the four areas of your life: work, health, family and learning.

■ Buy a large poster board, coloured pens, lots of magazines, glue, pins and tacks.

■ Sit quietly and ask yourself, 'What do I really want to achieve?'

■ Pick words that will be your theme for the coming year; for example, my theme this year is 'Focused Action'.

■ Go through magazines and cut out relevant pictures and words.

■ Lay out all the pictures and buzz words on the board.

■ If you are making a personal vision board then break the board into four areas: work, health, family and learning. Always put a picture of yourself in the centre of the board.

■ You can also encourage your team to use vision boards on your team away days.

■ Always start with the company name and logo in the centre and build the board and future vision from the centre.

■ Make a vision journal that you can take with you everywhere you go.

Motivation is an inside job

Motivation is an expression of harmony between what we feel inside about whatever we are doing on the outside. Before we can ever hope to motivate someone else we have first to motivate ourselves.

- Have a mantra or slogan you live by; for example, mine is 'Don't just talk about it. Just be it.'

- When you find yourself feeling demotivated nip it in the bud. Think of a moment in the past when you were really motivated.

- Take action, change your mindset, stop the pattern and feel yourself becoming inspired again.

- Encourage each and every member of your team to be 100% responsible.

- Write your own obituary and then live each day and every moment as if it was your last.

- Analyse setbacks; don't complain about them, just let them go.

- Make everyone around you feel valued.

Feel the fear, do it afraid

The only way to handle fear is to step into it. Then fear can no longer control you. When we do what we fear or face up to what we fear, the fear dissipates and we very often find it was our minds creating illusions of false expectations appearing real. When we grab hold of fear suddenly we feel excited and ready and it doesn't scare us any more.

- Identify your fear and take small steps every day.

- Say 'yes' to your fear and let it into your life.

- Stop talking about your fear; you are only encouraging it to live more in your mind.

- Know that ninety per cent of all your fears are imaginary.

- Choose happiness, take action and see it as a challenge you can overcome.

- Put your fear into perspective.

- If you don't give your fears energy you can watch them disappear from your life.

- Change your questioning approach; ask yourself, 'what can I learn from this fear?'

- Know that when you step into your fear it can no longer control you.

Tenacity

Tenacity is a great leadership muscle that can be developed. Tenacity is all about never giving up, no matter what. Leaders who have great tenacity understand that sometimes things take time to happen.

I learned the gift of tenacity at a very young age. At school the headmaster told me I was an empty vessel that made a lot of noise and throughout my teenage years I was bullied and called names. No matter how hard life became I held on to the idea that one day I would and could make a difference in the world.

- Never give up; be persistent.

- Consider the worst case scenario and take the risk.

- Tenacity is about staying focused.

- Do what you need to do so it will take you where you want to be.

- Know that most things in life take time to happen.

- Keep away from the nay-sayers. Cut them out of your life.

- Tenacity also means going with the flow and being flexible.

- Every day build your resilience and know that any good achievement requires effort.

Persistence

Persistence is the ability to keep going in times of change and anxiety. It is the ability to get up and keep on walking when the road ahead is foggy; as you walk through the fog the road will become clearer.

- Break your actions down into small steps.
- If you feel you're becoming overwhelmed stop and take a break.
- Carry a notebook and keep positive affirmations close by you.
- Focus on the present and the actions you can take in this moment.
- Be courageous and take action every day.
- Do three things every day that align with your current goals.
- Be personable and upbeat with everyone you meet.
- Every day keep improving.
- Be self-reliant and believe in your ability as a leader.

Transmit fear

Louis Gerstner turned around IBM when he found out that facts, fear and force don't motivate people. He realised that he had to create emotional equity with his people. The result was he turned around IBM as people started to feel valued in the workplace.

- You have got two ears and one mouth so listen twice as much as you talk.
- Communication isn't a solo endeavour; surround yourself with talented people.
- Offer your customers so much value that you leave them breathless.
- Be prepared to listen before sharing what you want people to know.
- Listening and empathising first earns you the right to share your information.
- Pause and have the patience to listen.
- Outstanding leaders share their beliefs with staff and colleagues.
- Have fun; having fun is one of the best means to connect in a real way.
- Focus on positive communication.
- Focus on team strengths.
- Build cooperative, close, vibrant relationships.
- It's OK to make mistakes (mistakes are to be learned from).

Clarity

By setting clear goals in the important areas of your life you begin to get more clarity in your life. Clarity precedes mastery. Clarity helps you move in the direction of your vision.

■ Know the ultimate purpose of your business. Revisit it every quarter with your team.

■ Know the role and purpose you fulfil in the business.

■ Every day rank yourself on a scale from 1 to 10 on how passionate you are about what you currently do.

■ Every morning and evening open your goals book and re-read the intentions you set.

■ Explore with your team how you turn information into insights and insights into ideas where action is taken.

■ Know the top three values that you live by.

■ Know what your personal purpose is and explore how that fits in with your current work.

■ Be clear about the key responsibilities of your role.

■ Find a mentor to take you to the next level.

Setbacks

Leaders know that setbacks are just a chance to pause and rethink a new solution. Leaders understand that there are many setbacks along the way. Learn to look for the opportunity in the setback and ask yourself the question, 'what is the opportunity that is emerging right now?' Perseverance is all important.

- Accept and deal with it.
- Change your mindset and stay positive.
- Focus on the future. The setback is in the past now.
- Teach others what you have learned.
- Know you are not the only one.
- Learn to see the setback as an opportunity for growth.
- Look back on past successes and know more are on their way.
- Never doubt yourself.
- Reassess your priorities and plan for the future.

Seconds to ponder ⏱

What do you really want in life?

....

....

If you had all the money in the world would you still have the same vision?

....

....

Why is it important to you as a leader?

....

....

How will you feel when you achieve it?

....

....

How will it help the world?

....

....

Are you owning and being 100% responsible for achieving these goals?

....

....

Are you focused on all the ways you can achieve it?

....

....

What legacy will you leave?

....

....

How would you like to be remembered?

....

....

How will you define success so you know when you have been successful?

....

....

What is the one step you can take now that will initiate this action plan?

....

....

What is the long view of your leadership plan?

....

....

What would you do this day if you knew you could not fail?

....

....

Seconds to action ⏱

What actions will you take?

....

....

....

....

....

....

....

....

....

....

....

....

....

....

....

....

....

....

....

....

....

....

....

....

....

....

Seconds review

Eight key lessons from chapter 6

1. Never let the fear of failure stop you from taking action.

2. When you are eighty per cent there just do it.

3. Take the next step and be there now.

4. What two things can you do by the end of today to take action?

5. Keep a goals journal.

6. Tape your goals and aspirations, play it in your car, listen to it on your phone.

7. Make a huge vision board and place it in your office as a constant reminder to take action every day.

8. Live each moment as if it were your last.

'To make positive changes in our lives we need a sense of future. Then we can move with focus in that direction.'

Molly Harvey

Conclusion

Now that you have come to the end of the book know that you are only ever seconds away from outstanding leadership. You can refer to the book at any time in the future. Treat it as a tool box of tips and strategies that you can use again and again.

I wish you much continued success on your journey to outstanding leadership and remember my motto: 'Don't talk about it; just be it'.

Molly Harvey

We need your help

Molly's vision is to reach 333 million people by 21st December 2020 at 3 p.m. with the *Seconds away from outstanding leadership* philosophy.

If you have been inspired by the book and want to help others stand in their own presence and lead with impact, listed below are some steps you can take.

Share your thoughts about the book on Facebook, Twitter, online book retailers and websites that you visit. If you have your own website why not blog about some of the points in *Seconds away from outstanding leadership*.

Buy extra copies of the book for friends, family and co-workers. They will learn that they are only ever seconds away from outstanding leadership.

If you are a CEO or manager invest in copies of the book for all your team.

Visit www.secondsawayfrom.com and join the worldwide movement today.

Free resources

You are only seconds away from outstanding leadership.

Now that you have finished reading *Seconds away from outstanding leadership* you are at a crossroads with two choices:

Choice one
You can make the *Seconds away from outstanding leadership* philosophy part of the resonance in your presence and lead with impact every day.

Choice two
Do nothing and put it up on your bookshelf with all the other leadership books.

To raise your game to a whole new level and create profound results I encourage you to take advantage of the free resources below within the next twenty-four hours.

www.secondsawayfrom.com

Free audio programme to help you implement the ideas in the book.
Seconds away from outstanding leadership gift book.
Join the online *Seconds away from outstanding leadership* movement.

www.mollyharvey.com

A full brochure and range of resources for personal and organisational leadership are available from www.mollyharvey.com including videos, podcasts, corporate tips, articles and Molly's blog.

To book Molly for a *Seconds away from outstanding leadership* presentation contact Brendan O'Connor at The London Speaker Bureau on +44 (0)20 8748 9595 or email Brendan@londonspeakerbureau.co.uk.

Follow Molly on Twitter or visit Molly on Facebook to learn more about her events, travels and community.